THE WEALTH MINDSET

The Wealth Mindset
Understanding the Mental Path to Wealth

Taught by
Neville Goddard

For more information visit:
<u>www.radicalcounselor.com</u>

The ideas, concepts, and opinions expressed in this book are intended to be used for educational purposes only. This book is made available with the understanding that the author and publisher are not presenting any specific medical or psychological advice. The author and publisher claim no responsibility to any person or entity for any liability, loss, or damage caused or alleged to be caused directly or indirectly as a result of the use, application, or interpretation of the material in this book.

ISBN-13: 978-1539612803
ISBN-10: 1539612805

Printed in the United States of America

"Assume you are what you want to be. Walk in that assumption and it will harden into fact."

Editor's Note

Neville Goddard (1905–1972) was one of the great self-improvement teachers of the 20th century. His strikingly practical interpretation of the Bible has helped thousands of people transform their lives, and remains some of the best spiritual advice ever recorded in American history.

Neville was a master at explaining how the Bible could be understood metaphysically. This three-part guide reveals several essential and underrated aspects of Neville's philosophy, taken from material he presented in 1953, at the peak of his speaking career. The first segment provides an introduction to Neville's fundamental teaching points from that time, originally published as part of a "New Thought" bulletin. The second and third sections are lectures Neville gave in Los Angeles, where he often spoke at Dr. Frederick Bailes' Science of Mind Church and the Ebell Theater. The material has been slightly edited for increased clarity. Enjoy.

– Tim Grimes

CONTENTS

PART ONE:
FUNDAMENTALS
Page 11

PART TWO:
CHANGING THE FEELING OF "I"
Page 18

PART THREE:
SOUND INVESTMENTS
Page 37

PART ONE:
FUNDAMENTALS

With so vast a subject, it's indeed a difficult task to summarize in a few hundred words what I consider the most basic ideas on which those who seek a true understanding of metaphysics should now concentrate. I shall do what I can in the shape of three fundamentals.

These fundamentals are:

- *Self-Observation*

- *Definition of Aim*

- *Detachment*

The purpose of true metaphysics is to bring about a rebirth or radical psychological change in the individual. Such a change cannot take place until the individual first discovers the self that he would change.

This discovery can be made only through an uncritical observation of his reactions to life.

The sum total of these reactions defines the individual's state of consciousness, and it's the individual's state of consciousness that attracts the situations and circumstances of his life. So the starting point of true metaphysics, on its practical side, is *self-observation* – in order to discover one's reactions to life, reactions that form one's secret self, the cause of the phenomena of life.

With Emerson, I accept the fact that: *"Man surrounds himself with the true image of himself...what we are, that only can we see."*

There's a definite connection between what is *outer* and what is *inner* in man, and it's always our inner states that attract our outer life. Therefore, the individual must always start with himself.

It's one's self that must be changed.

Man, in his blindness, is quite satisfied with himself, but heartily dislikes the circumstances and situations of his life. He feels this way, not knowing that the cause of his displeasure lies not in the condition nor the person with whom he's displeased, *but in the very self he likes so much*.

Not realizing that "he surrounds himself with the true image of himself" and that "what he is, that only can he see," he's shocked when he discovers that it's always been *his own deceitfulness* that made him suspicious of others.

Self-observation would reveal this deceitful one in all of us; and this must be accepted before there can be any transformation of ourselves. At this moment, try to notice your inner state. *To what thoughts are you consenting? With what feelings are you identified?* You must be ever careful of where you are within yourself. Most of us think that we're kind and loving, generous and tolerant, forgiving and noble – but an uncritical observation of our reactions to life will reveal a self that is *not at all* kind and loving, generous and tolerant, forgiving and noble.

And it's this self that we must first accept and then set about to change.

Rebirth depends on inner work of one's self. No one can be reborn without changing this self. Any time an entirely new set of reactions enters into a person's life, a change of consciousness has taken place; a spiritual rebirth has occurred.

Having discovered – through an uncritical observation of your reactions to life – a self that must be changed, you must now formulate an aim. *That is, you must define the one you would like to be instead of the one you truly are in secret.* With this aim clearly defined, you must – throughout your conscious waking day – notice your every reaction in regards to this aim. The reason for this is that everyone lives in a definite state of consciousness, that state of consciousness we've already described as the sum total of his reactions to life.

Therefore, in defining an aim, you're defining a state of consciousness – which, like all states of consciousness, must have its reactions to life. For example: if a rumor or an idle remark could cause an anxious reaction in one person and no reaction in another, this is positive proof that the two people are living in two different states of consciousness.

If you define your aim as being a noble, generous, secure, kindly individual – knowing that all things are states of consciousness – you can easily tell whether you're faithful to your aim in life by watching your reactions to daily events. If you're faithful to your ideal, your reactions will conform to your aim. For you'll be identified with your aim and, therefore, will be *thinking from* your aim. If your reactions aren't in harmony with your ideal, it's a sure sign that you're separated from your ideal and are only *thinking of* it. Assume that you're the loving one you want to be, and notice your reactions throughout the day in regards to that assumption.

For your reactions will tell you the state from which you're operating.

This is where the third fundamental – *detachment* – enters in. Having discovered that everything is a state of consciousness made visible – and having defined that particular state which we want to make visible – we now set about the task of *entering such a state*. For we must move psychologically from where we are to where we desire to be.

The purpose of practicing detachment is to separate us from our present reactions to life and attach us to our aim in life.

This inner separation must be developed by practice. At first, we seem to have no power to separate ourselves from undesirable inner states – simply because we've always taken every mood, every reaction, as natural and have become identified with them. When we have no idea that our reactions are only states of consciousness from which it's possible to separate ourselves, we go round and round in the same circle of problems – not seeing them as inner states, but as outer situations.

We practice detachment, or inner separation, so that we may escape from the circle of our habitual reactions to life. That's why we must formulate an aim and constantly notice ourselves in regard to that aim.

This teaching begins with *self-observation*. Secondly, it asks, *"What do you want?"* And then it teaches detachment from all negative states and attachment to your aim. This last state – attachment to your aim – *is accomplished by frequently assuming the feeling of your wish fulfilled*.

We must practice separating ourselves from our negative moods and thoughts in the midst of all the troubles and disasters of daily life. No one can be different from what he is now unless he begins to separate himself from his present reactions and to identify himself with his aim.

Detachment from negative states and assumption of the wish being fulfilled must be practiced in the midst of all the blessings and cursings of life.

The way of true metaphysics lies in the midst of all that is going on in life. We must constantly practice self-observation, thinking from our aim, and detachment from negative moods and thoughts, if we would be doers of truth instead of mere hearers.

Practice these three fundamentals and you'll rise to higher and higher levels of consciousness. Remember, always: *It is your state of consciousness that attracts your life.*

Start climbing!

– Neville

PART TWO:
__CHANGING THE FEELING OF "I"__

Let me give you a quick summary of the thought expressed here. We claim that the world is a manifestation of consciousness, that the individual's environment, circumstances, and conditions of life are only the out-picturing of the particular state of consciousness in which that individual abides.

Therefore, the individual sees whatever he is by virtue of the state of consciousness from which he views the world. Any attempt to change the outer world, before he changes the inner structure of his mind, is to labor in vain. Everything happens by order. Those who help or hinder us, whether they know it or not, are the servants of this law – which constantly shapes outward circumstances in harmony with our inner nature.

I ask you to distinguish between the individual identity and the state it occupies. The individual identity is the Son of God, and by that I really mean our imagination. That is permanent. Imagination fuses with a state and believes itself to be the state with which it's fused – but at every moment of time it's free to choose the state with which it'll be identified.

That brings us to today's subject – *Changing the Feeling of "I"* – and I hope I won't get the same reaction that's recorded in the sixth chapter of the Gospel of John. For we're told that when this was given to the world they all left Jesus, leaving just a handful behind. For when Jesus told them there was no one to change but self, they said this is a hard, hard teaching.

It's a hard thing. Who can hear it? For he said, *"No man cometh unto me save I call him."* And then it's recorded when he repeated it three times they left him, never again to walk with him. And he turned to the few who remained and asked them, *"Would you also go?"* And they answered and said, *"To whom would we go? You have the word of eternal life."*

In other words, it's so much easier when I can blame another for my misfortune. But now I'm told that no man cometh unto me save I call him, that I'm the sole architect of my fortunes and misfortunes.

It's a difficult saying. And so it's recorded, *"It's a hard saying. Who can hear it? Who can grasp it? And who will believe it?"*

And so later Jesus said, *"And now I sanctify myself that they also be sanctified through the truth."*

For if this is the truth, then there's no one to change – no one to make whole, no one to purify – but self. And so we start with the "I." Most of us are totally unaware of the self that we really cherish. We've never taken one good look at the self, so we don't know this self. For this "I" has neither face, form nor figure – but it does mold itself into structure by all that it consents to, all that it believes.

And few of us know really what we do believe. We have no idea of the unnumbered superstitions and prejudices that go to mold this inner, formless "I" into a form which is then projected as a man's environment, as the conditions of life. So here, read it carefully when you go home:

"No man cometh unto me save I call him." (John 6:44)

"You didn't choose me; I have chosen you." (John 15:16)

"No man can take away my life; I lay it down myself." (John 10:18)

There's no power to take from me anything that's part of the inner arrangement of my mind.

"All that you gave me I have kept and none is lost save the son of perdition." (John 17:12)

Or the belief in God. And because nothing can be lost but *the belief* in loss, I'll not now assume loss of anything you've given me that's good.

"And so I sanctify myself that they be sanctified through the truth." (John 17:19)

So now, how do we go about changing the "I"? First of all, we must discover the "I," and we do this by an uncritical observation of self. This will reveal a self that will shock you. You'll be altogether – I wouldn't say afraid – but *ashamed* to admit you've ever known such a lowly creature. And had it been God Himself who drew near in this despicable form, you'd have denied him a thousand times before a single cock would crow. You couldn't believe that this is the self that you've carried around and protected and excused and justified.

Then, you start changing this self after – by uncritical observation – you make the discovery of it. For the acceptance of self is the essence of the moral problem of the world. It's the epitome of a true outlook on life. *For it's the sole cause of everything you observe.* Your description of the world is a confession of the self that you don't know. You describe another, you describe society – you describe anything – and your description of the thing you observe reveals to one who knows this law the being *you really are*.

So you must first accept that self. When that self is accepted, then you can start to change. It's so much easier to take the virtues of the Gospel and apply them as the word of life: To love the enemy, to bless those who curse us, and to feed the hungry. But when man discovers the being to be fed, the being to be clothed, the being to be sheltered – the greatest enemy of all – *is himself*, then he is ashamed, completely ashamed.

That's the being.

It was easier to share with another something that I possess, to take an extra coat and give it to another...but when I know the truth, it's not that. I start with myself, having discovered the truth, and start with the changing of myself.

Now, let me tell you a story. A few years ago, in this city, I was giving a series of lectures down near that lake – I can't even recall the name of the lake, but it was some Parkview Manor where I spoke, and in that audience was a gentleman who sought an audience before the meeting. We went across the street into the little park there, and he said to me that he had an insoluble problem.

I said, "There's no such thing as an insoluble problem."

"But," he said, "you don't know my problem. It's not a state of health, I assure you. It's...look at the skin that I wear."

I said, "What's wrong with it? It looks lovely to me."

He said, "Look at the pigment of my skin. I, by the accident of birth, am now discriminated against. The opportunities for progress in this world are denied to me just because of the accident of birth, that I was born a colored man. Opportunities for advancement in every field, neighborhoods that I'd like to live in and raise a family, I can't move to. Where I'd like to open up a business, I can't move into that area."

Then I told him my own personal experience, when I came to this country. Well, I didn't have this same problem, but I was a foreigner in the midst of all Americans. I didn't find it difficult.

"Yet," he reminded me, "that's not my problem, Neville. Others have come here speaking with an accent, but they haven't my skin, and I was born an American."

→ Then I told him an experience of mine in New York City. If I were called upon to name a man that I'd consider my teacher, I'd name Abdullah. I studied with that gentleman for five years. He had the same color of skin, the same pigment as this gentleman. He would never allow anyone to refer to him as a colored man. He was very proud of being a negro, didn't want any modification of what God had made him.

Abdullah turned to me once and said, "Have you ever seen a picture of the Sphinx?" I said, "Yes." He said, "It embodies the four fixed quarters of the universe. You have the lion, the eagle, the bull and man. And here's man, that's the head. The crown of that creature called the Sphinx, which still defies man's knowledge to unriddle it, was crowned with a human head. And look carefully at the head, Neville, and you'll see whoever modeled that head must have been a negro. Whoever modeled it had the face of a negro and if that still defies man's ability to unravel it, I'm very proud that I'm a negro."

I've seen scientists, doctors, lawyers, bankers – from every walk of life – seek an audience with old Abdullah, and everyone who came thought themselves honored to be admitted to his home and to receive an interview. If he was ever invited out – and he was – he was always the honored guest. He told me, "Neville, you must first start with self. Find self, don't be ashamed ever of the being you are. Discover it and start the changing of that self."

Well, I told this gentleman exactly what Abdullah had taught me: that there was no cause outside of the arrangement of his own mind. If he was discriminated against, it wasn't because of the pigment of his skin, though he showed me signs as large as all outdoors denying him access to a certain area. The sign is there only because in the minds of some men, such patterns are formed and they draw unto themselves what now they would condemn.

There's no power outside the mind of man to do anything to man, and he by the arrangement of *his own* mind – by consenting to these restrictions in his cradle and being conditioned slowly through his youth, waking into manhood *believing* himself set upon – would have to be set upon.

But *"no man cometh unto me save I call him."*

So then someone comes to condemn, or to

praise. They couldn't come unless *I* call them. Not a man called Neville, but that secret being that's not called Neville. The secret being that's the sum total of *all* of my beliefs, *all* of the things that I consent to, that forms a pattern of structure. That secret being draws unto itself things in harmony with itself.

Well, that man went away and wrestled with himself. He couldn't believe everything I told him, not that night. But last Sunday morning in the lobby, he came forward and we renewed the friendship. He took me next door to show me the fruit of this teaching.

He said, "Neville, it took me almost three years to really overcome that fixed idea that I, by the accident of birth, would be a secondary citizen. But I overcame it. Now, here's my office on Wilshire Boulevard. I picked this one not because it was the only one offered – four equally wonderful spots were offered to me. I took this one because it had greater telephone facilities, but the others were equally good. Now, you couldn't judge my income from this office, lovely as it is. Everything is nice about it, but, Neville, this year I'll net a quarter of a million dollars."

Well, in America that's still a fabulous sum of

money. It would be staggering in any other part of the world, but even in fabulous America a man netting a quarter of a million is really up in the very highest of brackets. And that was the same man that a few years ago told me the whole vast world was against him by reason of the accident of birth. He knows now he is what he is by virtue of the state of consciousness with which he's identified. And the choice is his: to go back to the restrictions of his childhood, when he believed the story, or to continue in the freedom that he has found.

So you and I can be anything in this world we desire to be, if we'll clearly define our aim in life and constantly occupy that aim.

It must be habitual. The concept we hold of self that is noble must not be put on just for a moment and taken off when we leave this church. We feel free here; we feel that we have something in common, that's why we're here, but are we going to wear the noble concept we now hold of self when we go through the door and enter that bus, or are we going to return to the restrictions that were ours prior to coming here? The choice is ours and the hardest lesson to learn is that there's no one in this world that can be drawn into your world unless you – *and you alone* – call him.

So don't do what they did thousands of years ago, for that's the beginning of the secession of the great truth. We're told they turned away from it, never again to walk with it, and the few who remained didn't like it either, but where would they go if this is the word of eternal truth?

Not that it's true just for this day and age, but if this *is* the law of being – and in all the dimensions of my being it holds good – if this is eternally true, then let me learn the lesson now, though I wrestle with myself as this man did for three years.

So, changing the feeling of "I" is a selective thing, because unnumbered states are infinite states. But the "I" is not the state. The "I" believes itself to be the state when it enters and fuses with it, so this man was presented with a state early in life, and without the faculty of discrimination in his youth, he fused with the state and believed these restrictions were true. And it took him three years to disentangle the "I" from these fixed ideas with which he had lived for so many years.

Now, you may take only a moment – or you too may take three years. I can't tell you how long it's going to take you. But I'll tell you this much: *It can be measured by the feeling of naturalness*. You can wear a feeling until it's natural. The moment the feeling becomes natural, it'll begin to bear fruit within your world.

I told this story at a small gathering here in the city. Not many asked questions about it, but three people said: "But he must have had money before. He must have known the right people. He must in some way have had some substance to start it. Because how can you go out to loan a million dollars? And call that a real fact, that you have that to loan, and tell me you didn't have someone who had it? Or you, yourself, didn't already have it?"

I didn't ask this gentleman about the individual facts of the case. I went into his office. I saw it. I didn't look at his books. He volunteered this information, and gave me the figure of a quarter of a million net for the year. I haven't checked or in any way verified the statement; I believe it implicitly.

I'll not go along with those who believe that, unless you have certain things to start with, you can't apply this law. You can start now from scratch and choose the being you want to be. You aren't going to change the pigment of your skin, but you'll find your accent – or the pigment of skin, or your so-called "racial background" – will not be a hindrance. For if a man is ever hindered, it can only be *the state of consciousness in which he abides* that hinders him. Man is freed or constrained by the state of mind in which he persists. If you wish to persist in your current state, well, then persist in it.

But I warn you: *No one cares*.

And that's an awful blow when a man discovers that no one – *no one but himself* – really cares. We find ourselves weeping with ourselves in the hope of getting others to weep with us. And what an awful shock, when the day arrives, that we discover that no one really ever cared. They'll give us some little listening ear for a moment just as they were passing by, but they really didn't care. When we make that discovery, we shake ourselves out of it, and boldly appropriate the gift our Father gave us before the world was.

So let me show you the gift. You've read your Lord's Prayer, possibly daily, but you read it as a prayer from a translation of a translation, which doesn't reveal the sense of the original evangelist. The real translation you'll find in Farrar Fenton's work, where in the original it's written in the imperative passive mood – which is like a standing order, a thing to be done absolutely and continuously; so that you can look now upon your universe as one vast inter-knit machinery where all things happen. There isn't a thing to become. All things are *now* taking place, so it's written in this manner:

"Thy will must be being done. Thy kingdom must be being restored."

It's the only way you could express it if you would express the imperative passive mood. But from the Latin from which our translation was made, there's no first aorist of the imperative passive mood. So we have it in the way we have it, but it doesn't reveal the intent of the mysteries.

If you'll see all things are *now*, you don't become. You simply *select* the state that you would occupy. Occupying it, you become it *now*: it's already a fact, every aspect of that state in its most minute detail. It's worked out and taking place. You, by occupying the state, still seem to have to go through the action of unfolding that state – but the state is really now already completely finished and taking place.

So right now you can choose the being you want to be.

And by choosing a being other than what you're now expressing, you start to change the feeling of "I." Now, how will I know that I've changed the feeling of "I"? By beginning first with an uncritical observation of my reactions to life, and then noticing my reactions when I think I'm identified with my choice. If I assume that I'm the man that I want to be, let me observe my reactions. If they're as they were, I haven't identified myself with my choice. For my reactions are *automatic* – and so if I *am* changed I would automatically change my reactions to life. So changing the feeling of "I" results in a change of reaction; that change of reaction is a change of environment and behavior.

But let me warn you: *A little alteration of mood is not a transformation.*

It's not a real change of consciousness. Because if I change my mood for a moment it can quickly and rapidly be replaced by another mood in the reverse direction. When I say "changed" – as this gentleman changed his mood, his basic mood, his state of consciousness – it means assuming that I am *what the moment denies, what my reason denies*. And that I nonetheless remain in that assumed state long enough to make it stable, so that all of my energies are flowing from that state. I'm no longer thinking *of* that state. I'm thinking *from* that state.

So whenever a state grows so stable as to definitely expel all of its rivals, then that central, habitual state of consciousness from which I think defines my character and is really a true transformation, or change of consciousness.

Whenever I reach that state of stability, watch my world then mold itself in harmony with this inner change. And men will come into my world, people will come to aid me, and they'll think they're initiating the urge to help. But they're playing only their part. They must do what they do because I've done what I did. Having moved from one state into the other, I've altered my relationship relative to the world around about me, and that changed relationship compels a change in behavior relative to my world. So people *have* to act differently toward me.

So, in changing the "I," you start with desire. For it starts with desire. Desire is the spring of action, for you must want to be other than what you are. We fail because we don't fall in love enough with an ideal. We aren't, I would say, moved enough to want to be other than what we are. If I could get you to be completely in love with some state, to the point where it haunted the mind, I could almost prophesize that you would in the not distant future externalize that state within your world. And the reason we fail is we aren't hungry enough to change. For either we do not know this law, or we haven't the urge or the hunger to really bring about the change.

For changing of the feeling of "I" results in a change of reaction, and a change of reaction results in a change of the world. If you like your world, and you're complacent about it, you haven't started on the road of mysteries. For the very first beatitude appeals to one who isn't complacent: *"Blessed are the poor in spirit."*

You must be poor in spirit, not complacent, not satisfied.

The man who thinks that the reason of birth – the religion that he inherited at birth – is good enough for him, he isn't dissatisfied. He's not, I would say, moved. That being is complacent and, therefore, he isn't poor in spirit; he's very rich in spirit.

Theirs is not the kingdom of God. For if I could stir you – make you dissatisfied with self – then you'll recognize that self and set about to truly change it. For the only field of activity for man is within himself and on himself. You don't work on the other. <u>The day you change self, that day you change your world.</u>

So I hope that many of you are hungry. Even if you're stirred up trying to disprove what I told you, I'd accept that challenge. For in the attempt to disprove what I just told you, if you're sincere in your attempt, you would prove it.

It's important to define an aim in this world, to have a goal, for without an aim you're aimless. And you were warned in the Epistle of James that *"the double minded man is unstable in all his ways. Let not such a man believe that he shall receive anything of the Lord, for he is like a wave that is driven and tossed by the wind."*

That man never reaches his goal. So you must have an aim, and define your desire. There are certain schools who teach you to kill out desire; we teach you to *intensify* desire, and show you the reason for such teaching – show you what the Bible teaches about desire.

Let me remind you of a very simple technique. Any time that you exercise your imagination, and do it lovingly on behalf of another, you are mediating God to man. So, we sit quietly and we simply become imitators of our Father. And He called the world into being by being the thing He would call.

And so we sit and we listen as though we heard someone congratulating us on having found what we seek.

We *go to the end* of the matter and we listen just as though we heard. And we look as though we saw. And we try in this manner *to feel ourselves right into the situation of our answered prayer.*

And there we wait in silence for a few minutes.

So try this simple technique. If you want to clear your throat, please do so. If you want to shift your position in the chair to relax, do so. And I'll make you this promise: The day you're very still in mind and really become attentive, you'll hear coming from without what really you're whispering from within yourself.

PART THREE:
SOUND INVESTMENTS

Today's subject is "Sound Investments." I want to share with you today what I consider one of the truly great revelations of all time. On Sunday morning, April 12th, my wife woke from what was really a deep, profound sleep, and as she was waking a voice distinctly spoke to her. The voice spoke to her with great authority and said: *"You must stop spending your thoughts, your time, and your money. Everything in life must be an investment."*

So she quickly wrote it down and went straight to the dictionary to look up the two important words in the sentence: "spending" and "investing." The dictionary defines spending as *"to waste, to squander, to layout without return."* To invest is to *"layout for a purpose, for which a profit is expected."*

Then I began to analyze the sentence – "You must stop spending your thoughts, your time and your money, for everything in life must be an investment." As I dwelt upon it, I saw that everything is *now* – that through the portals of the present all time must pass – and this psychological *now*, the state in which I find myself now, does not recede into the past. It advances into my future.

So, what I do *now* is the all-important thing.

And thought is the coin of heaven. It's the money of heaven. So the thought I entertain now, the thought to which I consent, is as told to us in Ephesians: *"All things when they are admitted are made manifest by the light, and all things when they are manifested are light."*

The word "light" is defined as consciousness. So the state to which I consent must be made manifest. And when it is manifest, it's only that state of consciousness made visible, coming to bear witness of the state in which I abided.

So, every moment of time, I'm either spending or I'm investing. Unfortunately, most of us *spend* the coin of heaven – and morning, noon and night we live in negative states for which there's no return – when we could easily not have spent, but *invested* that moment, so at the end of the day we really would have a wonderful portfolio.

The religious minded person invests possibly on Sunday morning. Through the service he's lifted for a moment; if he's not overly critical he might be carried away with the hymn; he might be carried away with the solo, the organ music, the address from the pulpit, and for a moment he's investing. But the rest of the week he spends.

You know from experience, if you put all your money into one great concern, it may be wonderful and sound, but at the end of a year, the directors may decide to reorganize and to pass a dividend. If you depended on that dividend check for your daily needs – though it's a good, firm, wonderful concern – when they decided to pass on it, then you must either sell some stock, or raise or borrow on it.

But every moment of time you can have a most marvelous portfolio. And if they pass a dividend, it doesn't matter. Devote every moment of your time to positive thinking – constructive thinking – by not accepting any rumor that doesn't contribute to the fulfillment of your desire. No matter what it is – it could be the most obvious fact in the world – <u>if it doesn't contribute to the fulfillment of your dreams, don't accept it</u>. If you do, you're spending.

If, not by denying, but by *complete indifference* – complete non-acceptance – you turn to what you wish you could've heard instead of what you heard, you're investing.

It's not the hearing that matters; it's the admitting the truth of it that matters. "All things when they are admitted" – not all things when they are heard. But if you give consent to it – if you accept it as true – then you either *spend by acceptance* or *you invest depending on the nature of the state accepted.*

So, this revelation, which came through my wife to me, is one of the greatest that I've heard. Had it been told in our Bible, it would've been told in its strange meter: "And the Lord God spoke unto her this day and said to her…" They would have told what revelation would have come in that manner. But it came to a normal, natural wife; came in a normal, natural manner…to instruct not only her, but to instruct her husband.

For I was the first one to whom she told it, and I can't tell you what it has done to me since I heard it on the morning of the 12th of April. For it made me more aware of the moment, made me far more conscious of every moment of the day, so that I'm not spending. *I must invest*. Time is too precious and these moments don't recede. They don't pass away. They're always advancing into my future to either confront me with a waste, or to show me some wonderful return.

If I invest it's for a purpose and, therefore, I hope – not only hope – I *expect* a reward. I expect a profit on my investment. So a moment spent now, this very day, could tomorrow pay you great dividends. I told a story here two weeks ago of Jimmie Fuller. Well, I didn't have all the details of the story, but dozens of you said to me after my meetings at the Ebell Theatre, that to have made the fortune that he made, he must have had great capital.

Well, I could neither affirm nor deny your bold assertion, for you spoke as though you knew. And many of you almost convinced me that he had great capital, and that's why he turned it into great returns. So, last Friday at the Ebell, I saw Jimmie and asked him to tell me more of the details. He said, "When you came here four years ago, Neville, I came to hear you. My wife asked me, 'Why do you go to hear Neville? Who told you of Neville?'"

He went on and explained, "I turned the radio on one night and I heard Dr. Bailes. I'd never heard of the man before. At the end of his lecture, which I thoroughly enjoyed, he said Neville is coming to speak to us and it's a *must*. Well, I so liked Dr. Bailes that I turned him on the next night, and for the next two weeks he kept on promoting you, and he was so generous in his praise, I thought, 'I've got to hear this man.' So when you came, I enjoyed what I heard on Sunday morning, and then you announced you were speaking the following night at this place, but it was two dollars."

"Well," he said, "I actually had fifty-four dollars, and a wife and a little boy. We couldn't leave the little child alone, he was a baby, so it meant a sitter. But my wife and I came to everything you gave, and one night, we couldn't pay the sitter; we just didn't have it, but we took our last money and came to your every meeting – the two of us. And one night we didn't have money to pay that sitter. Three years later, Neville, I hadn't proven your theory. You know my problem, as I told you before."

Perchance there is someone here who didn't hear it – Jimmie is a negro, and his problem was that because he was a negro, all the marks and stripes of the world were against him. I tried to convince him it was only in his own mind that these stripes were placed; his acceptance of that as restriction made it restriction, and if he could only *drop it* by non-acceptance – by complete indifference to the pigment of skin – he could accomplish his every dream by acceptance of it *now*.

Well, in the last year, Jimmie Fuller, by complete acceptance, investing his moment – *his now* – has turned the year into a net profit of two hundred and fifty thousand dollars. He didn't have one penny when he started. He didn't raise large capital. He didn't have it. He only invested God's coin. God gave it to him. He gave him *the moment*, which is time. So instead of spending his thought and his time thinking he had no money – which everyone does – he knew that thought *was* money.

So he invested his thought in the now.

He knew that his thought wasn't going to recede and vanish from sight; that it was an investment: It would advance into his future. Well, it did. It so advanced that he tells me now everything he touches turns to gold. He has three children now; they come here every Sunday to Sunday school. He doesn't want his children to start with his stripes, so he wants them to feel what this Church gives. Jimmie tells me many a Sunday he feels like taking off for the beach or up to the mountains with his wife, but he won't go because he wants his children to have an opportunity he didn't have.

He told me, "My people were very religious,

but they must have worshipped a very poor God, for they were steeped in poverty. So I just wouldn't go near the churches of my mother and my brothers and these people, because I couldn't conceive of such a God doing that to us – yet they never missed service. When I found what I found here in this Science of Mind Church, I brought my children to Sunday School.

"Now this is what happened to them. Here, God is love, and love surrounds them and they know nothing but love, that God is love. One day my little girl which is the youngest of the three, was quite sick, a beastly cold. And that night, when the little boys said their prayers, these are the words they used: 'Thank you God, that sister is perfect tomorrow.' They couldn't look at the little girl, sick as she was, and say 'Thank you God, that sister is well now,' but they said, 'Thank you, God, that sister is perfect tomorrow.' Neville, it was a miracle. The next day, that child was perfect; there wasn't any sign of a cold – a complete absence of all that we saw the night before, and these two little brothers simply gave thanks.

"Now, one of my boys wanted a watch. I wouldn't give him the watch. I could've bought a thousand watches for him. But I want my little son to learn a law which I didn't know until recently. So he filled his mind with the possession of a watch, and he spoke of the watch as a 'live' watch – one that ticks, one that's alive, not a toy watch. So then he filled his mind with the possession of the watch. Then on his way to school he found a 'live' watch.

"Now he knows the working of the law: That the complete acceptance of the state in consciousness must result in an externalization of the state accepted. So if he accepts the watch, he doesn't need to turn to his earthly father as the medium through which the watch will come. I don't want to think for one second he has to point to his mother or his father as the only channels through which his good will come. I want him to recognize an Infinite Father – *the Father of us all* – who gave to him as He gave to me everything that I'll accept.

"I want my children to learn it as I have learned. Yes, I could shower them with gifts, but then they'd look to me as the only channel through which it will come. That I must not accept. So you should see the little boys and little girl actually live by this law. God to them is love and the only reality, and love surrounds them. So they never miss the Sunday School here."

Then he went on to tell me all the other

wonderful things that have happened by the mere acceptance of this law. He said, "The getting of my car, this convertible Cadillac – I treated it loosely. I sat quietly in my living room and imaginatively drove my Cadillac, and I simply treated it loosely. I didn't put real effort into it, I accepted it and then when I decided to get it I simply put in three telephone calls and that day I was driving this car, Neville.

"Now *everything* happens just like that. Today, instead of going to my office and working in the office, I work behind the scenes. I sit all day and I hear the report that's good from my employees. My entire office staff *must* tell me good news – it's the only thing I'll allow myself to hear. I ride my car...I'm in the office...I'm at home...I'm in the office...*but I'm only hearing good news*. And seldom do I go to the office physically to do office work. I'm behind the scenes only hearing good news.

"So I've completely forgotten the so-called pigment of skin, Neville. And honestly I can tell you today I feel that I'm blessed beyond all men because I was born a negro. I'm so proud to be born a negro. I'm so proud I am one."

And here's another part of his story that will interest all of you. Jimmie told me, "I had some property to dispose of. I had certain things in investments for those who had money, so I advertised them and a man called me on the wire. He saw the ad, and asked me if I was the gentlemen, so I told him I was the one who had the property. The first thing he said to me was, 'I don't want any nigger property.'"

Jimmie continued, "I didn't answer. As if I hadn't even heard the word. If he wants to be prejudiced, he may be prejudiced, that's his right. He wants to be silly about it, that's his right. He can spend; he need not invest. So I said, 'It's perfectly all right, sir, I have all kinds of property, I have all kinds of things for your investment.' A week later he called me up and said, 'Would you come and see me?' So I went to see him. When I got out of my car, his knees almost buckled – for he didn't know a negro was coming to see him, and a negro walked up his stairs into his living room.

"Within a matter of minutes, he purchased $37,000 worth of property that I had to offer. He said the first $25,000 that he bought he simply bought to buy back his face, and then the remaining $12,000 he bought because it was a very good investment. Well, since that time, this gentleman has spent tens of thousands of dollars with me and constantly calls to thank me because they're such wonderful investments."

Now, here's a man who is proud of his skin. Jimmie has no prejudices, because that's spending time he can't afford to spend. So in harmony with the revelation given to my wife, let us all now stop spending our thoughts, our time, and our money.

For everything in our life must be an investment.

We know the truth. This platform radiates the truth. You're told that everything proceeds out of your own consciousness, and that what you and you alone accept as true will externalize and mold itself in your environment. All the conditions that you'll encounter will simply bear witness to the state you've accepted. Well, if you don't like what you're encountering, then stop spending and learn the art of investment. For every moment of time is an opportunity to invest, not to spend.

Yet, on the other hand, you and I are free – we're free to waste every coin in the world. For that we have a right. We're free beings: we can spend; we need not invest. But if you know you can invest, why not choose the wiser way? We're told in the thirtieth chapter of the Book of

Deuteronomy, *"The commandment I command you this day is not hidden, and it isn't far off. It's near unto thee; it is in thy mouth and in thy heart. Now, I set before you this day, life and good, death and evil, blessings and cursings. Choose life, choose blessing."*

But the choice is ours, for we're free. He sets before us this day, this very moment, a commandment. He sets everything before us – it's not far away, it's in our tongue right now. And before me now is a blessing or a curse. I can accept the fact you don't like me – it doesn't matter, you may actually love me – but if I accept the fact that you don't like me and don't like the teaching, I'm spending my time. Tomorrow you'll prove to me that I've spent my time by your behavior relative to me. On the other hand, if I accept the fact that you do like it, because you're proving it, then I'd have no doubt in my mind that you couldn't do anything other than contribute to this teaching.

So it's up to me to either bless myself or curse myself.

I can choose life or I can choose death. I can choose the good. But I'm free – I can choose the evil. It's entirely up to me. But if you and I love this, accept it and believe it, then we're wise indeed if – knowing the whole is before us – we go out determined to become investors, not spenders. Not wasting and squandering our substance, but laying it out for a purpose.

Every moment, become conscious of that moment. What are you doing? I'm accepting now the fact that I'm a noble, dignified, wonderful being – that my Father is proud of the son who is like Him. So I'll not hear or accept as true anything other than that which contributes to that noble concept I hold of myself. I'll see that I'm secure. And maybe a headline would startle the world, but I'll not accept it. For if I don't admit to it, it can't proceed out of me. For all things when they are admitted are made manifest, none unless they are admitted.

So if I *now* will admit I'm using this moment as my moment to invest in my ideal – if I admit I am what reason denies, what my senses deny – I proceed in that assumption, knowing that, even though it doesn't confirm itself tonight or tomorrow, I'll still live in the assumption that I am what I want to be. And all day I'll tune in and listen only for the good report. I know these are investments, and tomorrow these dividend checks must come. *They must come.* That's the law of our being.

So everyone here, take it to heart, and know

you don't need money. To the hundreds of you who said to me in private, "He must have had money," I now know the story. I didn't know it when you boldly claimed that he must have had money, but now I have it from the source. Jimmie Fuller only had fifty-four dollars. And the fifty-four dollars were spent coming to my meetings, even when he couldn't spend a dollar on a sitter. So I tell you he didn't have it – yet he has it today. But you don't need even fifty-four dollars. All you need is time and you have it: *It's now*.

All you need is the thought. That's money.

So instead of spending the thought in the now, invest the thought in the now. For your *now*, this very moment as I stand here – and I'll get off the platform in a little while and you'll think now he's gone and he'll come back next year – doesn't go. What I'm doing now isn't going to slip away. It's going to move forward and embody itself as a condition, embody itself as the circumstance of my life. My *now's* – my reactions to what I'm hearing and saying and seeing, all of my reactions – are spelling out my tomorrow.

So I'll repeat it, through the doorway of *now*. Because Jesus said, *"I am the door."* "I am" is always first person present. Not I was the door, or I will be the door – *"I am the door," "I am the resurrection."* So what I do in the present, now, isn't going to recede. It's going to advance into my future. For through the door of the present – of the now – all time must pass. Don't spend it as it passes through the door of the now, invest it. Every moment of your life. See that it's a positive, constructive, noble moment. I promise you a wonderful, healthy, radiant future if you'll invest the now in such a way.

When a man learns the art of thinking from the end, that man is master of his fate. For he defines his end, he formulates an aim in life, and then feels himself right into the situation of that end.

So he thinks *from* it instead of thinking *of* it. The average man defines his dreams, but he remains back here looking at them because he's thinking *of* them. The wise man occupies the state of his dreams, so he radiates from it, he thinks *from* it. To use this little illustration: I'm standing here looking out at the auditorium, and I'd describe this theater based on this angle, for I'm seeing it from the stage. You – sitting in the auditorium or the balcony – you're looking at the theater from that angle, and that's how you see it. So the difference between us is we see the same theater from different angles. I'd define it from here; you'd define it from there. If I desired to get your point of view – while still standing here – *I'd assume that I'm seated where you are and within my imagination look from that position.* I'd then see the stage, not the auditorium. I'd describe the theater from the position that I'm assuming I am.

If the imagined position represents one of security, and my former position one of insecurity, I'd now assume that I am secure. And to prove that I am, I'd then look from the state of security, and I'd describe the world relative to my assumption. If I'm now still seeing what I saw when I was insecure, I haven't succeeded in occupying that desirable end. I'm still only thinking of it.

So the wide difference between thinking *from* and thinking *of* must be clearly seen. And then understand the wisdom in learning the art of thinking *from* a desired end. Look out at your world, formulate your lovely aims in life, and just ask yourself, *"What would it be like were it true that I now embody that state? How would I feel?"*

In response to that question comes a feeling, a positive feeling that corresponds to that end. Learn *to think from that end* – though reason denies it, though everything denies it. You occupy that end. It's *now*, you're investing in it, and it'll become real within your world.

Another point that I want to make clear is what Jimmie Fuller told me was one of the cues in his success: When the action of the inner man corresponds to the action the outer man must take in order to appease his desire, he'll definitely realize his desire. There are two of us; there's an inner man and an outer man. The outer man is always made to say, *"I of myself can do nothing. The Father within me, this inner one, He doeth the work. What I see Him do, I the outer, do also."*

So there's an inner you.

I can sit here now and immobilize my body – by relaxing it – and imagine what the outer me would have to do in order to appease my desire. While relaxed, just let me imagine that *I am actually it now*. So I keep the body immobilized, but I imagine that I'm actually experiencing the fulfillment of my desire now. And I'll experience in my imagination that which I would have to experience in the flesh to appease my desire.

Then I imagine that state over and over and over – *so that the actions of the inner man correspond to the actions the outer takes, fulfilling his desire.*

When that's done...I promise you it's going to be done in the flesh, too. No power in the world could stop it when these two actions coincide, but let it always spring from the inner you. Right now, we can do this. Know that any time we exercise our imagination lovingly on behalf of another, we're actually and literally mediating God to man. So we can sit quietly in the darkness and simply listen as though we heard the good report that we want to hear.

We look into the darkness and imagine we're seeing what we want to see.

This is investing the next two minutes. We've taken the moments that make up two minutes, and invest it now. So when I sit down in this chair and the lights are lowered, let's listen and let's look as though we're hearing and seeing what we want to hear and see. And we're actually fulfilling the command of that wonderful voice that spoke to my wife when it said to her, *"You must stop spending your time, your thoughts, and your money. For everything in life must be an investment."*

Let these two minutes be your greatest investment.

Part of the
NEVILLE EXPLAINS THE BIBLE
Series

Other books in the *Neville Explains the Bible* series include:

RELAX MORE, TRY LESS

THE POWER OF AWARENESS

MANIFESTATION THROUGH RELAXATION

FEELING IS THE SECRET

LAW OF ATTRACTION SUCCESS STORIES

MINDFUL MANIFESTATION

MANIFESTING MIRACLES

FREEDOM FOR ALL

Taught by Neville Goddard
Edited by Tim Grimes

For more information visit:
www.radicalcounselor.com

Made in the USA
Middletown, DE
26 June 2021